SLEEP
WELL

Vicky Bureau

A Crabtree Roots Plus Book

Crabtree Publishing
crabtreebooks.com

School-to-Home Support for Caregivers and Teachers

This book helps children grow by letting them practice reading. Here are a few guiding questions to help the reader with building his or her comprehension skills. Possible answers appear here in red.

Before Reading:

• What do I think this book is about?
  - *I think this book is about why sleep is important.*
  - *I think this book is about how sleep helps me grow.*

• What do I want to learn about this topic?
  - *I want to learn about how sleep helps my mind.*
  - *I want to learn about how sleep helps my body.*

During Reading:

• I wonder why...
  - *I wonder why sleep helps me stay healthy and happy.*
  - *I wonder how sleep helps me grow.*

• What have I learned so far?
  - *I have learned that sleeping well is a healthy habit.*
  - *I have learned that sleep helps your body rest.*

After Reading:

• What details did I learn about this topic?
  - *I have learned why sleep is important.*
  - *I have learned that even fish and insects sleep.*

• Read the book again and look for the vocabulary words.
  - *I see the word **rest** on page 7 and the word **dream** on page 14. The other vocabulary words are found on page 23.*

Sleeping well is a healthy **habit**.

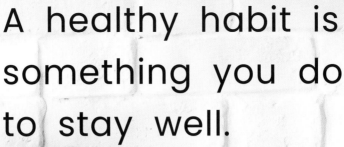

A healthy habit is something you do to stay well.

After a long day, sleep helps you **recharge**.

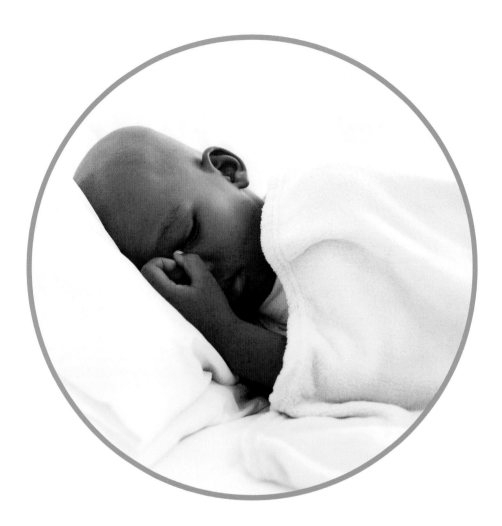

Sleep helps your body **rest**.

Sleep helps your body **repair**.

Sleep helps your body restore.

Sleep helps your body refresh.

Sleep helps your body **reenergize**!

Sleep helps you rest after today.

And prepare for tomorrow.

Sometimes you **dream**
when you sleep.

Do you remember your last dream?

Everybody sleeps.

You sleep. I sleep.

Animals sleep.

Even fish and insects sleep!

Sleep keeps us healthy.

Sleep is a healthy habit!

Word List
Sight Words

after	helps	sleep
animals	insects	something
body	long	stay
day	prepare	today
everybody	refresh	tomorrow
fish	remember	well
healthy	restore	your

Words to Know

dream

habit

recharge

reenergize

repair

rest

SLEEP
WELL

Written by: Vicky Bureau

Designed by: Kathy Walsh

Series Development: James Earley

Proofreader: Melissa Boyce

Educational Consultant: Marie Lemke M.Ed.

Photographs:

Shutterstock: Cover: MillaF, Mochipet; pg 3 & 23 Nina Buday; pg 4 Rawpixel.com; pg 6 OlgaKhorkova; p 7 & 23 michaeljung; pg 8 & 23 Rido; pg 9 Rawpixel.com; pg 10 & 23 Yuganov Konstantin; pg 11 & 23 LightField Studios; pg 12 Olesia Bilkei; pg 13 Monkey Business Images; pg 14 & 23 Yuganov Konstantin; pg 15 Africa Studio; pg 16 Sergey Novikov; pg 18 Erik Lam; pg 19 New Africa; pg 20 Brocreative; pg 21 Hung Chung Chih

Crabtree Publishing

crabtreebooks.com   800.387.7650

Printed in the U.S.A./072023/CG20230214

Published in Canada
Crabtree Publishing
616 Welland Ave
St. Catharines, Ontario
L2M 5V6

Published in the United States
Crabtree Publishing
347 Fifth Ave
Suite 1402-145
New York, NY 10016

Library and Archives Canada Cataloguing in Publication
Available at Library and Archives Canada

Library of Congress Cataloging-in-Publication Data
Available at the Library of Congress

Hardcover: 978-1-0398-0986-4
Paperback: 978-1-0398-1039-6
Ebook (pdf): 978-1-0398-1145-4
Epub: 978-1-0398-1092-1